Shopping

Around the World

Clare Lewis

raintree
a Capstone company — publishers for children

CARDIFF
CAERDYDD

Raintree is an imprint of Capstone Global Library Limited, a company incorporated in England and Wales having its registered office at 7 Pilgrim Street, London, EC4V 6LB – Registered company number: 6695582

www.raintreepublishers.co.uk
myorders@raintreepublishers.co.uk

Edited by Joanna Issa, Shelly Lyons, Diyan Leake and Helen Cox Cannons
Designed by Cynthia Akiyoshi
Original illustrations © Capstone Global Library Ltd 2014
Picture research by Elizabeth Alexander and Tracy Cummins
Production by Victoria Fitzgerald
Originated by Capstone Global Library Ltd
Printed and bound in China

ISBN 978 1 406 28200 9 (hardback)
18 17 16 15 14
10 9 8 7 6 5 4 3 2 1

ISBN 978 1 406 28207 8 (paperback)
19 18 17 16 15
10 9 8 7 6 5 4 3 2 1

British Library Cataloguing in Publication Data
A full catalogue record for this book is available from the British Library.

Acknowledgements
We would like to thank the following for permission to reproduce photographs: Getty Images pp. 5 (Otto Stadler), 7 (Michael Avina), 9 & 22e (both Anthony Pidgeon), 12 & 23a (both William Andrew), 13 (MachineHeadz), 16 (lillisphotography), 18 (Michael DeYoung), 21 (Image Source); Shutterstock pp. 1 (© Brenda Carson), 2 (© Isabella Pfenninger), 3 (© Natali Glado), 8 (© ValeStoc), 14 (© AJP), 17 (© Lakov Filimonov), 19 (© steve estvanik); Superstock pp. 6 (Blend Images), 4 & 22c (both Michael Nolan/Robert Harding Picture Library), 10, 22a & 23b (all Stefano Politi /age footstock), 11 (Ian Cumming/Axiom Photographic/Design Pics), 15 & 22d (both Egon Bömsch/ imagebrok /imagebroker.net), 20 & 22b (both Nano Calvo/ age footstock).

Cover photograph of a floating market in Bangkok, Thailand, reproduced with permission of Alamy (© Jan Wlodarczyk).

Every effort has been made to contact copyright holders of material reproduced in this book. Any omissions will be rectified in subsequent printings if notice is given to the publisher.

All the internet addresses (URLs) given in this book were valid at the time of going to press. However, due to the dynamic nature of the Internet, some addresses may have changed, or sites may have changed or ceased to exist since publication. While the author and publisher regret any inconvenience this may cause readers, no responsibility for any such changes can be accepted by either the author or the publisher.

Contents

Shopping everywhere

All over the world, people go shopping.

People buy things they need.

People use money to buy things.

Different countries have different money.

Where do people go shopping?

People go to shops.

Some shops are big.

Some shops are small.

People go to markets.
Some markets are inside.

Some markets are outside.

Some people shop on the internet.

The shopping is delivered to their door.

What do people buy?

People go shopping to buy food.

People go shopping to buy clothes.

People go shopping to buy toys.

People go shopping to buy things
for their homes.

Getting the shopping home

Some people carry their shopping in bags.

Some people carry their shopping
on their heads.

Shopping is different all around the world.

Where do you go shopping?

Map of shopping around the world

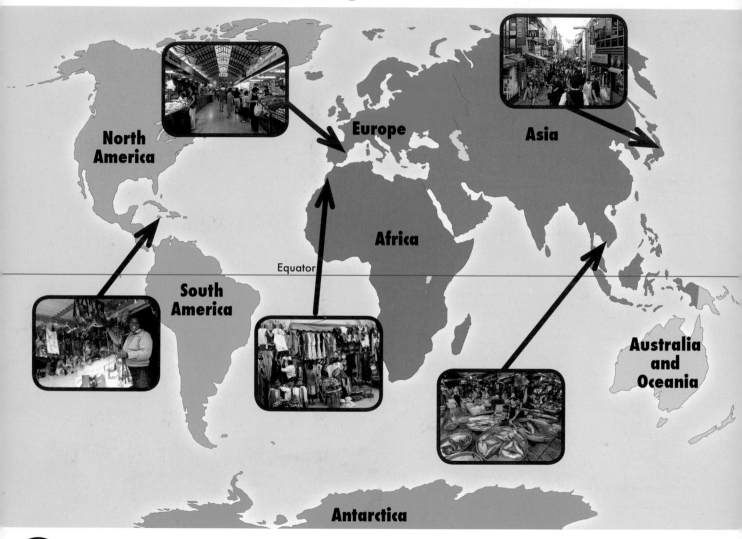

North
America

South
America

Equator

Europe

Africa

Asia

Australia
and
Oceania

Antarctica

Picture glossary

internet way of using computers that allows people who are far away to share information

market place where people buy and sell things. Many markets have small shops or stalls.

Index

Notes for parents and teachers
Before reading

Ask children about the last time they went shopping with someone. Where did they go? What did they buy? How did they pay for it? Show children the title and the contents page. Read the entries and explain that the contents page is a tool to help readers know what information is in the book and where to find it. Ask children to predict what they will learn from this title after reading the contents page.

After reading

- Turn to page 12 and read the sentence. Ask children if they know what *internet* means. Do any clues in the photograph help them know? Then turn to the glossary on page 23 and explain that a glossary is a tool that helps explain some of the more difficult words in the book. Find and read the definition for *internet*.

- Point out the map on page 22 and demonstrate how to use the map to identify the continents on which different photos from the book were taken. Ask children where the photo on page 15 was taken (Morocco/Africa). Have children look at the details in the photo. What is being sold? Have they ever seen a market outdoors like this? What is similar and different between this market and the places where they go shopping?